D1621025

The Birth of Christ

NELSON/REGENCY

Nashville

Contents

Introduction

The story of Christ's birth shows us just how simple, straightforward, and unaffected God is willing to be in order to accomplish His will on earth and meet human needs. There is nothing vain or unnecessary about it. The same can be said of the gospel. Jesus came to the earth, lived His life as an example, paid the price for our complete salvation, and imparted the very life and nature of God to all who would receive it.

The Christmas story reveals the miracle of God's great love for us.

�֍ ✿ ✿ ✿ ✿ ✿ ✿ ✿ ✿ ✿ ✿ ✿ ✿ ✿ ✿ ✿

JESUS CHRIST IS BORN
Matthew 1

18

Now the birth of Jesus Christ was as follows: After His mother Mary was betrothed to Joseph, before they came together, she was found with child of the Holy Spirit.

19

Then Joseph her husband, being a just man, and not wanting to make her a public example, was minded to put her away secretly.

20

But while he thought about these things, behold, an angel of the Lord appeared to him in a dream, saying, "Joseph, son of David, do not be afraid to take to you Mary your wife, for that which is conceived in her is of the Holy Spirit.

21

"And she will bring forth a Son, and you shall call His name J*ESUS*, *for He will save His people from their sins."*

22

So all this was done that it might be fulfilled which was spoken by the Lord through the prophet, saying:

23

"Behold, the virgin shall be with child, and bear a Son, and they shall

call His name Immanuel," which is translated, "God with us."

24

Then Joseph, being aroused from sleep, did as the angel of the Lord commanded him and took to him his wife,

25

and did not know her till she had brought forth her firstborn Son. And he called His name JESUS.

The Birth and Life of Christ Foretold

THE SEED OF A WOMAN

Genesis 3

15

"And I will put enmity
Between you and the woman,
And between your seed and her
Seed;
He shall bruise your head,
And you shall bruise His heel."

❖ ❖ ❖ ❖ ❖ ❖ ❖ ❖ ❖ ❖ ❖ ❖ ❖ ❖ ❖

A DESCENDANT OF ABRAHAM
Genesis 12

3

"I will bless those who bless you,
And I will curse him who
curses you;
And in you all the families of
the earth shall be blessed."

❀ ❀ ❀ ❀ ❀ ❀ ❀ ❀ ❀ ❀ ❀ ❀ ❀ ❀

A DESCENDANT OF ISAAC
Genesis 17

19

Then God said: "No, Sarah your wife shall bear you a son, and you shall call his name Isaac; I will establish My covenant with him for an everlasting covenant, and with his descendants after him."

A DESCENDANT OF JACOB
Numbers 24

17
"I see Him, but not now;
I behold Him, but not near;
A Star shall come out of Jacob;
A Scepter shall rise out of Israel,
And batter the brow of Moab,
And destroy all the sons of
tumult."

❀ ❀ ❀ ❀ ❀ ❀ ❀ ❀ ❀ ❀ ❀ ❀ ❀ ❀

FROM THE TRIBE OF JUDAH
Genesis 49

10

The scepter shall not depart
* from Judah,*
Nor a lawgiver from between
* his feet,*
Until Shiloh comes;
And to Him shall be the
* obedience of the people.*

✼ ✼ ✼ ✼ ✼ ✼ ✼ ✼ ✼ ✼ ✼ ✼ ✼ ✼ ✼

HEIR TO THE THRONE OF DAVID
Isaiah 9

7

*Of the increase of His
government and peace
There will be no end,
Upon the throne of David and
over His kingdom,*

❀ ❀ ❀ ❀ ❀ ❀ ❀ ❀ ❀ ❀ ❀ ❀ ❀ ❀

To order it and establish it with judgment and justice
From that time forward, even forever.
The zeal of the LORD of hosts will perform this.

ANOINTED AND ETERNAL
Psalm 45

6

Your throne, O God, is forever and ever;
A scepter of righteousness is the scepter of Your kingdom.

7

You love righteousness and hate wickedness;

Therefore God, Your God, has anointed You
With the oil of gladness more than Your companions.

❀❀❀❀❀❀❀❀❀❀❀❀❀❀❀❀

ANOINTED AND ETERNAL
Psalm 102

25

*Of old You laid the foundation
of the earth,
And the heavens are the work
of Your hands.*

26

*They will perish, but You will
endure;*

❧ ❧ ❧ ❧ ❧ ❧ ❧ ❧ ❧ ❧ ❧ ❧ ❧ ❧ ❧ ❧

Yes, they will all grow old like a
    garment;
Like a cloak You will change
    them,
And they will be changed.

27

But You are the same,
And Your years will have
    no end.

✠✠✠✠✠✠✠✠✠✠✠✠✠✠✠✠

BORN IN BETHLEHEM

Micah 5

2

"But you, Bethlehem Ephrathah,
Though you are little among
the thousands of Judah,
Yet out of you shall come forth
to Me
The One to be Ruler in Israel,

❀ ❀ ❀ ❀ ❀ ❀ ❀ ❀ ❀ ❀ ❀ ❀ ❀ ❀ ❀

*Whose goings forth are from
of old,
From everlasting.*"

❀ ❀ ❀ ❀ ❀ ❀ ❀ ❀ ❀ ❀ ❀ ❀ ❀ ❀ ❀ ❀

TIME FOR HIS BIRTH
Daniel 9

25

"Know therefore and understand,
That from the going forth of
the command
To restore and build Jerusalem
Until Messiah the Prince,
There shall be seven weeks and
sixty-two weeks;

❀ ❀ ❀ ❀ ❀ ❀ ❀ ❀ ❀ ❀ ❀ ❀ ❀ ❀ ❀

The street shall be built again,
and the wall,
Even in troublesome times."

TO BE BORN OF A VIRGIN
Isaiah 7

14
"Therefore the Lord Himself will give you a sign: Behold, the virgin shall conceive and bear a Son, and shall call His name Immanuel."

❊ ❊ ❊ ❊ ❊ ❊ ❊ ❊ ❊ ❊ ❊ ❊ ❊ ❊ ❊

SLAUGHTER OF CHILDREN
Jeremiah 31

15

Thus says the LORD:

"A voice was heard in Ramah,
Lamentation and bitter weeping,
Rachel weeping for her children,
Refusing to be comforted for her
children,
Because they are no more."

FLIGHT TO EGYPT

Hosea 11

1
"When Israel was a child, I loved
him,
And out of Egypt I called My
son."

❀❀❀❀❀❀❀❀❀❀❀❀❀❀❀❀

THE WAY PREPARED
Isaiah 40

3

*The voice of one crying in the
wilderness:*
"Prepare the way of the LORD;
Make straight in the desert
A highway for our God.

4

Every valley shall be exalted

❀ ❀ ❀ ❀ ❀ ❀ ❀ ❀ ❀ ❀ ❀ ❀ ❀ ❀

And every mountain and hill
    brought low;
The crooked places shall be
    made straight
And the rough places smooth;

5

The glory of the LORD shall be
    revealed,
And all flesh shall see it
    together;
For the mouth of the LORD has
    spoken."

❧ ❧ ❧ ❧ ❧ ❧ ❧ ❧ ❧ ❧ ❧ ❧ ❧ ❧ ❧

PRECEDED BY A FORERUNNER
Malachi 3

1

"Behold, I send My messenger,
And he will prepare the way
*   before Me.*
And the Lord, whom you seek,
Will suddenly come to His
*   temple,*

Even the Messenger of the
covenant,
In whom you delight.
Behold, He is coming,"
Says the LORD *of hosts.*

❋ ❋ ❋ ❋ ❋ ❋ ❋ ❋ ❋ ❋ ❋ ❋ ❋ ❋ ❋

DECLARED THE SON OF GOD
Psalm 2

7

"I will declare the decree:
The LORD has said to Me,
'You are My Son,
Today I have begotten You.'"

❀ ❀ ❀ ❀ ❀ ❀ ❀ ❀ ❀ ❀ ❀ ❀ ❀ ❀

GALILEAN MINISTRY
Isaiah 9

1

Nevertheless the gloom will not
    be upon her who is distressed,
As when at first He lightly
    esteemed
The land of Zebulun and the
    land of Naphtali,
And afterward more heavily
    oppressed her,

❀ ❀ ❀ ❀ ❀ ❀ ❀ ❀ ❀ ❀ ❀ ❀ ❀ ❀

By the way of the sea, beyond
    the Jordan,
In Galilee of the Gentiles.

2

The people who walked in
    darkness
Have seen a great light;
Those who dwelt in the land of
    the shadow of death,
Upon them a light has shined.

❧ ❧ ❧ ❧ ❧ ❧ ❧ ❧ ❧ ❧ ❧ ❧ ❧ ❧ ❧ ❧

TO BIND UP THE
BROKENHEARTED
Isaiah 61

1

"The Spirit of the Lord GOD is
upon Me,
Because the LORD has anointed
Me
To preach good tidings to the
poor;
He has sent Me to heal the
brokenhearted,

*To proclaim liberty to the
  captives,
And the opening of the prison
  to those who are bound;*

2

*To proclaim the acceptable year
  of the LORD,
And the day of vengeance of
  our God;
To comfort all who mourn."*

Gabriel Appears
to Zacharias

LUKE 1

5

There was in the days of Herod, the king of Judea, a certain priest named Zacharias, of the division of Abijah. His wife was of the daughters of Aaron, and her name was Elizabeth.

6

And·they were both righteous before God, walking in all the command-

❈ ❈ ❈ ❈ ❈ ❈ ❈ ❈ ❈ ❈ ❈ ❈ ❈ ❈ ❈ ❈

ments and ordinances of the Lord blameless.

7

But they had no child, because Elizabeth was barren, and they were both well advanced in years.

8

So it was, that while he was serving as priest before God in the order of his division,

9

according to the custom of the priest-hood, his lot fell to burn incense when he went into the temple of the Lord.

10

And the whole multitude of the people was praying outside at the hour of incense.

11

Then an angel of the Lord appeared

❀ ❀ ❀ ❀ ❀ ❀ ❀ ❀ ❀ ❀ ❀ ❀ ❀ ❀ ❀

to him, standing on the right side of
the altar of incense.

12

And when Zacharias saw him, he
was troubled, and fear fell upon him.

13

But the angel said to him, "Do not
be afraid, Zacharias, for your prayer
is heard; and your wife Elizabeth
will bear you a son, and you shall
call his name John.

14

"And you will have joy and gladness, and many will rejoice at his birth.

15

"For he will be great in the sight of the Lord, and shall drink neither wine nor strong drink. He will also be filled with the Holy Spirit, even from his mother's womb.

16

"And he will turn many of the children of Israel to the Lord their God.

17

"He will also go before Him in the spirit and power of Elijah, 'to turn the hearts of the fathers to the children,' and the disobedient to the wisdom of the just, to make ready a people prepared for the Lord."

❀ ❀ ❀ ❀ ❀ ❀ ❀ ❀ ❀ ❀ ❀ ❀ ❀ ❀

18

And Zacharias said to the angel, "How shall I know this? For I am an old man, and my wife is well advanced in years."

19

And the angel answered and said to him, "I am Gabriel, who stands in the presence of God, and was sent to speak to you and bring you these glad tidings.

❀ ❀ ❀ ❀ ❀ ❀ ❀ ❀ ❀ ❀ ❀ ❀ ❀ ❀ ❀ ❀

20

"But behold, you will be mute and not able to speak until the day these things take place, because you did not believe my words which will be fulfilled in their own time."

21

And the people waited for Zacharias, and marveled that he lingered so long in the temple.

❀ ❀ ❀ ❀ ❀ ❀ ❀ ❀ ❀ ❀ ❀ ❀ ❀ ❀ ❀

22

But when he came out, he could not speak to them; and they perceived that he had seen a vision in the temple, for he beckoned to them and remained speechless.

23

So it was, as soon as the days of his service were completed, that he departed to his own house.

24

Now after those days his wife Elizabeth conceived; and she hid herself five months, saying,

25

"Thus the Lord has dealt with me, in the days when He looked on me, to take away my reproach among people."

Gabriel Sent to Mary

26

Now in the sixth month the angel Gabriel was sent by God to a city of Galilee named Nazareth,

27

to a virgin betrothed to a man whose name was Joseph, of the house of David. The virgin's name was Mary.

28

And having come in, the angel said

❀ ❀ ❀ ❀ ❀ ❀ ❀ ❀ ❀ ❀ ❀ ❀ ❀ ❀ ❀

to her, "Rejoice, highly favored one,
the Lord is with you; blessed are you
among women!"

29

But when she saw him, she was
troubled at his saying, and consid-
ered what manner of greeting this
was.

30

Then the angel said to her, "Do not

✻ ✻ ✻ ✻ ✻ ✻ ✻ ✻ ✻ ✻ ✻ ✻ ✻ ✻ ✻

be afraid, Mary, for you have found favor with God.

31

"And behold, you will conceive in your womb and bring forth a Son, and shall call His name JESUS.

32

"He will be great, and will be called the Son of the Highest; and the Lord God will give Him the throne of His father David.

33

"And He will reign over the house of Jacob forever, and of His kingdom there will be no end."

34

Then Mary said to the angel, "How can this be, since I do not know a man?"

35

And the angel answered and said to her, "The Holy Spirit will come

❀ ❀ ❀ ❀ ❀ ❀ ❀ ❀ ❀ ❀ ❀ ❀ ❀ ❀ ❀

upon you, and the power of the Highest will overshadow you; therefore, also, that Holy One who is to be born will be called the Son of God.

36

"Now indeed, Elizabeth your relative has also conceived a son in her old age; and this is now the sixth month for her who was called barren.

37

"For with God nothing will be impossible."

38

Then Mary said, "Behold the maidservant of the Lord! Let it be to me according to your word." And the angel departed from her.

Mary Visits
Elizabeth

LUKE 1

39

Now Mary arose in those days and went into the hill country with haste, to a city of Judah,

40

and entered the house of Zacharias and greeted Elizabeth.

41

And it happened, when Elizabeth heard the greeting of Mary, that the

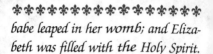

babe leaped in her womb; and Elizabeth was filled with the Holy Spirit.

42

Then she spoke out with a loud voice and said, "Blessed are you among women, and blessed is the fruit of your womb!

43

"But why is this granted to me, that the mother of my Lord should come to me?

44

"For indeed, as soon as the voice of
your greeting sounded in my ears,
the babe leaped in my womb for joy.

45

"Blessed is she who believed, for there
will be a fulfillment of those things
which were told her from the Lord."

The Magnificat
(Mary's Song)

46

And Mary said:

"My soul magnifies the Lord,

47

And my spirit has rejoiced in God my Savior.

48

For He has regarded the lowly state of His maidservant;

For behold, henceforth all generations will call me blessed.

49

For He who is mighty has done great things for me,
And holy is His name.

50

And His mercy is on those who fear Him
From generation to generation.

51

He has shown strength with His arm;
He has scattered the proud in the imagination of their hearts.

52

He has put down the mighty from their thrones,
And exalted the lowly.

53

He has filled the hungry with
good things,
And the rich He has sent away
empty.

54

He has helped His servant Israel,
In remembrance of His mercy,

55

As He spoke to our fathers,
To Abraham and to his seed
  forever."

56

And Mary remained with her about
three months, and returned to her
house.

John the Baptist Is Born

LUKE 1

57

Now Elizabeth's full time came for her to be delivered, and she brought forth a son.

58

When her neighbors and relatives heard how the Lord had shown great mercy to her, they rejoiced with her.

59

So it was, on the eighth day, that

❅ ❅ ❅ ❅ ❅ ❅ ❅ ❅ ❅ ❅ ❅ ❅ ❅ ❅ ❅

they came to circumcise the child;
and they would have called him by
the name of his father, Zacharias.

60

His mother answered and said, "No;
he shall be called John."

61

But they said to her, "There is no
one among your relatives who is
called by this name."

❋ ❋ ❋ ❋ ❋ ❋ ❋ ❋ ❋ ❋ ❋ ❋ ❋ ❋

62

So they made signs to his father—
what he would have him called.

63

And he asked for a writing tablet,
and wrote, saying, "His name is
John." So they all marveled.

64

Immediately his mouth was opened
and his tongue loosed, and he spoke,
praising God.

65

Then fear came on all who dwelt around them; and all these sayings were discussed throughout all the hill country of Judea.

66

And all those who heard them kept them in their hearts, saying, "What kind of child will this be?" And the hand of the Lord was with him.

Zacharias's
Prophecy

67

Now his father Zacharias was filled with the Holy Spirit, and prophesied, saying:

68

*"Blessed is the Lord God of Israel,
For He has visited and redeemed
His people,*

69

*And has raised up a horn of
salvation for us*

❀ ❀ ❀ ❀ ❀ ❀ ❀ ❀ ❀ ❀ ❀ ❀ ❀ ❀ ❀

*In the house of His servant
David,*

70

*As He spoke by the mouth of
His holy prophets,
Who have been since the world
began,*

71

*That we should be saved from
our enemies*

✿ ✿ ✿ ✿ ✿ ✿ ✿ ✿ ✿ ✿ ✿ ✿ ✿ ✿ ✿

*And from the hand of all who
hate us,*

72

*To perform the mercy promised
to our fathers
And to remember His holy
covenant,*

73

*The oath which He swore to
our father Abraham:*

✣ ✣ ✣ ✣ ✣ ✣ ✣ ✣ ✣ ✣ ✣ ✣ ✣ ✣ ✣ ✣

74

To grant us that we,
Being delivered from the hand of
*   our enemies,*
Might serve Him without fear,

75

In holiness and righteousness
*   before Him all the days of*
*   our life.*

❀ ❀ ❀ ❀ ❀ ❀ ❀ ❀ ❀ ❀ ❀ ❀ ❀ ❀

76

*"And you, child, will be called
the prophet of the Highest;
For you will go before the face
of the Lord to prepare His
ways,*

77

*To give knowledge of salvation
to His people
By the remission of their sins,*

❧ ❧ ❧ ❧ ❧ ❧ ❧ ❧ ❧ ❧ ❧ ❧ ❧ ❧ ❧

78

*Through the tender mercy of
our God,
With which the Dayspring from
on high has visited us;*

79

*To give light to those who sit in
darkness and the shadow of
death,
To guide our feet into the way
of peace.''*

80

So the child grew and became strong in spirit, and was in the deserts till the day of his manifestation to Israel.

The Birth of Jesus

❊ ❊ ❊ ❊ ❊ ❊ ❊ ❊ ❊ ❊ ❊ ❊ ❊ ❊

LUKE 2

1

And it came to pass in those days that a decree went out from Caesar Augustus that all the world should be registered.

2

This census first took place while Quirinius was governing Syria.

3

So all went to be registered, everyone to his own city.

4

Joseph also went up from Galilee, out of the city of Nazareth, into Judea, to the city of David, which is called Bethlehem, because he was of the house and lineage of David,

5

to be registered with Mary, his betrothed wife, who was with child.

6

So it was, that while they were there,

the days were completed for her to be delivered.

7

And she brought forth her firstborn Son, and wrapped Him in swaddling cloths, and laid Him in a manger, because there was no room for them in the inn.

The Angels and
the Shepherds

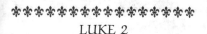
8

Now there were in the same country shepherds living out in the fields, keeping watch over their flock by night.

9

And behold, an angel of the Lord stood before them, and the glory of the Lord shone around them, and they were greatly afraid.

❀ ❀ ❀ ❀ ❀ ❀ ❀ ❀ ❀ ❀ ❀ ❀ ❀ ❀ ❀

10

Then the angel said to them, "Do not be afraid, for behold, I bring you good tidings of great joy which will be to all people.

11

"For there is born to you this day in the city of David a Savior, who is Christ the Lord.

12

"And this will be the sign to you:

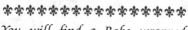

You will find a Babe wrapped in swaddling cloths, lying in a manger."

13

And suddenly there was with the angel a multitude of the heavenly host praising God and saying:

14

*"Glory to God in the highest,
And on earth peace, goodwill toward men!"*

15

So it was, when the angels had gone away from them into heaven, that the shepherds said to one another, "Let us now go to Bethlehem and see this thing that has come to pass, which the Lord has made known to us."

16

And they came with haste and found Mary and Joseph, and the Babe lying in a manger.

17

Now when they had seen Him, they made widely known the saying which was told them concerning this Child.

18

And all those who heard it marveled at those things which were told them by the shepherds.

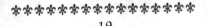

19

But Mary kept all these things and pondered them in her heart.

20

Then the shepherds returned, glorifying and praising God for all the things that they had heard and seen, as it was told them.

Simeon and Anna

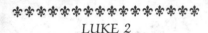

LUKE 2

21

And when eight days were completed for the circumcision of the Child, His name was called Jesus, the name given by the angel before He was conceived in the womb.

22

Now when the days of her purification according to the law of Moses were completed, they brought Him to Jerusalem to present Him to the Lord

23

(as it is written in the law of the Lord, "Every male who opens the womb shall be called holy to the LORD"),

24

and to offer a sacrifice according to what is said in the law of the Lord, "A pair of turtledoves or two young pigeons."

25

And behold, there was a man in Jerusalem whose name was Simeon, and this man was just and devout, waiting for the Consolation of Israel, and the Holy Spirit was upon him.

26

And it had been revealed to him by the Holy Spirit that he would not see death before he had seen the Lord's Christ.

27

So he came by the Spirit into the temple. And when the parents brought in the Child Jesus, to do for Him according to the custom of the law,

28

he took Him up in his arms and blessed God and said:

29

"Lord, now You are letting Your

servant depart in peace,
According to Your word;

30
For my eyes have seen Your
salvation

31
Which You have prepared before
the face of all peoples,

32
A light to bring revelation to
the Gentiles,

❊ ❊ ❊ ❊ ❊ ❊ ❊ ❊ ❊ ❊ ❊ ❊ ❊ ❊ ❊

*And the glory of Your people
Israel."*

33

*And Joseph and His mother mar-
veled at those things which were spoken of Him.*

34

*Then Simeon blessed them, and said
to Mary His mother, "Behold, this
Child is destined for the fall and*

❊ ❊ ❊ ❊ ❊ ❊ ❊ ❊ ❊ ❊ ❊ ❊ ❊ ❊ ❊ ❊

rising of many in Israel, and for a
sign which will be spoken against

35

(yes, a sword will pierce through your
own soul also), that the thoughts of
many hearts may be revealed."

36

Now there was one, Anna, a proph-
etess, the daughter of Phanuel, of the
tribe of Asher. She was of a great

❀ ❀ ❀ ❀ ❀ ❀ ❀ ❀ ❀ ❀ ❀ ❀ ❀ ❀ ❀ ❀

age, and had lived with a husband
seven years from her virginity;

37

and this woman was a widow of
about eighty-four years, who did not
depart from the temple, but served
God with fastings and prayers night
and day.

38

And coming in that instant she gave
thanks to the Lord, and spoke of Him

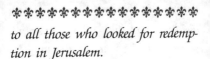

to all those who looked for redemption in Jerusalem.

39

So when they had performed all things according to the law of the Lord, they returned to Galilee, to their own city, Nazareth.

40

And the Child grew and became strong in spirit, filled with wisdom; and the grace of God was upon Him.

The Wise Men Come

1

Now after Jesus was born in Bethlehem of Judea in the days of Herod the king, behold, wise men from the East came to Jerusalem,

2

saying, "Where is He who has been born King of the Jews? For we have seen His star in the East and have come to worship Him."

✿ ✿ ✿ ✿ ✿ ✿ ✿ ✿ ✿ ✿ ✿ ✿ ✿ ✿ ✿ ✿

3

When Herod the king heard this, he was troubled, and all Jerusalem with him.

4

And when he had gathered all the chief priests and scribes of the people together, he inquired of them where the Christ was to be born.

5

So they said to him, "In Bethlehem

❊ ❊ ❊ ❊ ❊ ❊ ❊ ❊ ❊ ❊ ❊ ❊ ❊ ❊ ❊

of Judea, for thus it is written by the prophet:

6

'But you, Bethlehem, in the land of Judah,
Are not the least among the rulers of Judah;
For out of you shall come a Ruler
Who will shepherd My people Israel.' "

7

Then Herod, when he had secretly called the wise men, determined from them what time the star appeared.

8

And he sent them to Bethlehem and said, "Go and search carefully for the young Child, and when you have found Him, bring back word to me, that I may come and worship Him also."

❊ ❊ ❊ ❊ ❊ ❊ ❊ ❊ ❊ ❊ ❊ ❊ ❊ ❊ ❊

9

When they heard the king, they departed; and behold, the star which they had seen in the East went before them, till it came and stood over where the young Child was.

10

When they saw the star, they rejoiced with exceedingly great joy.

11

And when they had come into the

house, they saw the young Child with Mary His mother, and fell down and worshiped Him. And when they had opened their treasures, they presented gifts to Him: gold, frankincense, and myrrh.

12

Then, being divinely warned in a dream that they should not return to Herod, they departed for their own country another way.

Instructions
Through
Dreams

13

Now when they had departed, behold, an angel of the Lord appeared to Joseph in a dream, saying, "Arise, take the young Child and His mother, flee to Egypt, and stay there until I bring you word; for Herod will seek the young Child to destroy Him."

14

When he arose, he took the young

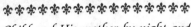

Child and His mother by night and departed for Egypt,

15

and was there until the death of Herod, that it might be fulfilled which was spoken by the Lord through the prophet, saying, "Out of Egypt I called My Son."

16

Then Herod, when he saw that he was deceived by the wise men, was

❊ ❊ ❊ ❊ ❊ ❊ ❊ ❊ ❊ ❊ ❊ ❊ ❊ ❊ ❊ ❊

exceedingly angry; and he sent forth and put to death all the male children who were in Bethlehem and in all its districts, from two years old and under, according to the time which he had determined from the wise men.

17

Then was fulfilled what was spoken by Jeremiah the prophet, saying:

❉ ❉ ❉ ❉ ❉ ❉ ❉ ❉ ❉ ❉ ❉ ❉ ❉ ❉

18

"A voice was heard in Ramah,
Lamentation, weeping, and
great mourning,
Rachel weeping for her children,
Refusing to be comforted,
Because they are no more."

19

Now when Herod was dead, behold,
an angel of the Lord appeared in a
dream to Joseph in Egypt,

20

saying, "Arise, take the young Child and His mother, and go to the land of Israel, for those who sought the young Child's life are dead."

21

Then he arose, took the young Child and His mother, and came into the land of Israel.

22

But when he heard that Archelaus

was reigning over Judea instead of his father Herod, he was afraid to go there. And being warned by God in a dream, he turned aside into the region of Galilee.

23

And he came and dwelt in a city called Nazareth, that it might be fulfilled which was spoken by the prophets, "He shall be called a Nazarene."

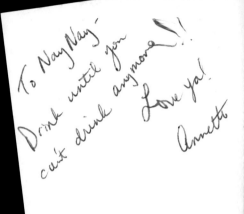

To Nay Nay -
Drink until you
can't drink anymore !!!
Love ya!
Annette

Wine Spectator's

Little Book of Wine

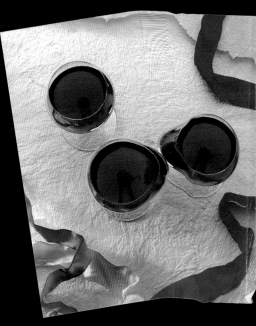

Wine Spectator's

Little Book of Wine

M. Shanken
Communications, Inc.
New York

RUNNING PRESS
PHILADELPHIA · LONDON

A Running Press Miniature Edition™

© 1999 by M. Shanken Communications, Inc.

Library of Congress Cataloging-in-Publication Number 98-68473

ISBN 0-7624-0653-4

M. Shanken Communications, Inc.
387 Park Avenue South
New York, NY 10016

This book may be ordered by mail from Running Press.
Please include $1.00 for postage and handling.
But try your bookstore first!

Running Press Book Publishers
125 South Twenty-second Street
Philadelphia, PA 19103-4399

Visit us on the web!
www.winespectator.com
www.runningpress.com

Contents

Preface

No one knows which culture was the first to make wine, but we do know that over the centuries, wine has meant many things to many peoples: The Greeks worshiped it in the guise of the god Dionysius; the Romans thought it a necessary accompaniment to any banquet;

and in medieval England, it played the role of a primitive medicine. Today, wine is enjoyed mostly as a purely aesthetic pleasure, yet it continues to inspire and to fascinate.

Over the past few years, more people than ever have adopted wine drinking as part of their lifestyles. While appreciation of its sensuous and intellectual gifts have remained constant throughout the years, only recently is wine once again being given its due as a healthy pleasure. The message we're hearing is that, when drunk in moderation, wine is not just an enjoyable beverage, but a healthful one as well.

In this small book, *Wine Spectator* has compiled a wealth of inspiring, thought-provoking comments articulated by some of the world's greatest thinkers, artists, and winemakers. From Euripedes to Julia Child, Julio Iglesias to Galileo Galilei, and Robert Mondavi to Andrew Lloyd Webber, wine lovers throughout history share their insights and philosophies on the joys that a fine wine can bring.

Perhaps Plato was right when he called wine a gift from the gods. A simple beverage, a marvelous dinner partner, a work of art; wine is a treasure in so many ways. To me, wine is about enjoying the company of friends, colleagues, and family. It's about rejoicing in the best life has to offer.

Cheers.

Marvin R. Shanken
Editor and Publisher,
Wine Spectator

Gold in the Glass

Where there is
no wine, love perishes,
and everything else that
is pleasant to man.

Euripides (484–407 B.C.)
Greek playwright

It is the finest of all French wines.
. . . I had thought it was lost to us
forever . . . a wine as rare and as
rich as happiness itself . . . of multiple
and mysterious tastes, a wine of the
mind and of the body. . . .

John le Carré
English writer

Home is where the wine is.

Michael Caine
English actor and restaurateur

The hunt for great wine values is an enjoyable sport. It means getting more pleasure for your money than you would normally expect.

Marvin R. Shanken
American editor and publisher

Wine is light held together by moisture.

Galileo Galilei (1564–1642)
Italian astronomer and physicist

Wine to me is passion. It's family and friends. It's warmth of heart and generosity of spirit. Wine is art. It's culture. It's the essence of civilization and the art of living.

from *Harvests of Joy* by Robert Mondavi, American winery owner

Wine cheers the sad, revives the old, inspires the young, makes weariness forget his toil, and fear her danger, opens a new world when this, the present, palls.

Lord Byron (1788–1824)
English poet

Tasting Tip

The shape and size of a wine glass can affect the way a wine tastes. The best wine glass is a slender goblet with a long stem on a sturdy base. The glass should hold ten to eighteen ounces, and the bowl should be biggest at the bottom, tapering to a small opening in order to concentrate the wine's aromas.

I see my wine life and my film life as being inextricably linked. I can unequivocally earn a decent living in film now, but I will never give wine up. It means too much to me.

Jonathan Nossiter
American filmmaker and wine consultant

One may dislike carrots, spinach, beetroot, or the skin on hot milk. But not wine. It is like hating the air one breathes, since each is equally indispensable.

Marcel Aymé (1902–1967)
French writer

Nothing more excellent
or valuable than wine
has ever been granted by
the gods to man.

Plato (427–347 B.C.)
Greek philosopher

Every serious wine lover be-
comes a wine taster at some
point. To fully appreciate
wine, you need to learn to taste it,
not just drink it.

Marvin R. Shanken
American editor and publisher

Tasting Tip

The best way to taste a wine is as follows.
First, hold the wine in your mouth, purse
your lips and inhale gently through them.
This action accelerates vaporization,
intensifying the wine's aromas. Next,
chew the wine vigorously, sloshing it

around in your mouth, to draw out every last nuance of flavor. After swallowing, exhale slowly through both your nose and mouth. The better the wine, the more complex, profound, and long-lasting the residual aromas will be.

Invariably, when I go visit other art collectors, they generally have a substantial wine collection, or they are at least very interested in fine wines. I think wine, to a large degree, is a work of art.

Norman Braman
American businessman and art collector

A bottle of good
wine, like a good act,
shines ever in the
retrospect.

Robert Louis Stevenson (1850–1894)
Scottish writer

I guess you could say I'm the ultimate fan of wine, rather than a connoisseur. I'm an amateur, but I've started to become really gung ho on the subject. I love the adventure of taste.

Itzhak Perlman
Israeli concert violinist

Music is a psychological landscape, with all sorts of indefinable things. Wine is the same way. It has tastes that are very hard to define. When I drink a great wine, I get a sense of breadth—it's like a chord sounding and echoing.

Michael Tilson Thomas
American symphony conductor

The best part of my new marriage—
this should make you jealous—is that
Erich has one of the greatest wine
cellars of all time!

American actress Paulette Goddard
(1911–1990) to ex-husband
Burgess Meredith after marrying
writer Erich Remarque

Good Storage Advice

If you collect fine wines that benefit from additional maturation, proper storage is essential. Wine bottles are best stored on their sides, either in cases or racked, in a cool, dark space with a constant temperature.

What I love about wine is
the joy of discovery.
It's the fact that wine is so
obviously affected by
what people do to create it.

Sir Andrew Lloyd Webber
English musical theater composer

Wine is more guts than brain.

Thomas Schmidheiny
Swiss businessman and winery owner

A Healthy Pleasure

I drink almost only red wine, and I'm absolutely convinced that it makes me much healthier.

Rudolph Giuliani
American politician

Wine makes daily living easier, less hurried, with fewer tensions, and more tolerance.

Benjamin Franklin (1706–1790)
American statesman

O thou invisible spirit of wine!

If thou hast no name to be known by,

let us call thee devil!

Cassio

Come, come; good wine is a good
familiar creature if it be well used;
exclaim no more against it.

Iago

From *Othello* by
William Shakespeare (1564-1616)
English playwright

Wine-Buying Strategy

As a general rule, most white wines, and very many reds, are best drunk within three years of the vintage; wines that age well increase in price over time. Beware of old, inexpensive wines.

Healthy or sick, I have drunk wine almost every night for the last twenty-five years. Sometimes a glass, sometimes a bottle, sometimes at a wine tasting. But always some wine, somehow.

Julio Iglesias
Spanish singer

Serving Tip

While the "correct" temperature at which to serve a wine is ultimately a matter of personal preference, most people use the following time-tested guidelines. Sparkling wines, dessert wines, and light-bodied whites should be served chilled to preserve their freshness and fruitiness. Fuller-bodied whites such as Chardonnays and white Rhônes may be served slightly warmer. Light reds like Beaujolais, Pinot Noir, and Cabernet Franc from the Loire Valley benefit from being served slightly cooler than full-bodied reds such as Australian Cabernet and Shiraz, California Cabernet and Meritage blends, and Bordeaux and Rhône reds, which are best served at cellar temperature (55 to 65 degrees Fahrenheit).

In Europe we thought of wine as something healthy and normal as food and also a great giver of happiness and well-being and delight. Drinking wine was not a snobbism nor a sign of sophistication nor a cult; it was as natural as eating and to me as necessary.

Ernest Hemingway (1899–1961)
American writer

Tasting Tip

Besides stirring up the full range of a wine's colors, swirling a glass of wine helps intensify its aromas. The easiest way to swirl is to rest the base of the glass on a table, hold the stem between thumb and forefinger and gently rotate the wrist. Move the glass until the wine is dancing, climbing nearly to the rim, then stop.

Wine from long habit has become indispensable to my health. Good wine is a necessity of life for me.

Thomas Jefferson (1743–1826)
American statesman

Wine . . . one sip
of this will bathe the
drooping spirits
in delight beyond the
bliss of dreams.
Be wise and taste.

John Milton (1608–1674)
English poet

From the Grape
to the Glass

The discovery of
a new vineyard does more
for the happiness of
mankind than the discovery
of a new star.

Anthelme Brillat-Savarin (1755–1826)
French gastronome

At first there's nothing but a sour bunch of beads hanging down. Time passes, the sun ripens them, they become as sweet as honey, and then they're called grapes. We trample on them; we extract the juice and put it into casks; it ferments on its own, it's become wine! It's a miracle!

Nikos Kazantzakis (1885–1957)
Greek poet and writer

Winemakers aren't what makes wine. Wine makes itself from the vineyard. All we are, are wine-watchers.

Jess Jackson
American winery owner

I am absolutely fascinated by the vineyards—the idea of seeing the grapes flower and ripen. How can one not find it interesting?

Baroness Philippine de Rothschild
French winery owner

It comes down to trying to find out what each wine should be. If you can figure out what this vineyard or what this grape wants you to do with it, you can make a great wine out of any variety.

Helen Turley
American vintner

We picked grapes all day long. When the tubs were filled, they weighed almost a hundred pounds. We were tired when the day was done, but we laughed and sang along the way.

Alsatian grape-picker

To make very good wine is to dream it. It is not necessary to be next to the vats and say, "I want to make wine, I want to make wine." I know the wine, I feel it.

Gérard Depardieu
French actor

Serving Suggestion

Should you decant a wine; that is, pour it from the bottle into a different container for serving? Yes, if the wine has thrown a heavy deposit; vintage Port and full-bodied, mature reds are the usual culprits here. Before decanting, the bottle should be upright for a minimum of twenty-four hours for best results.

The wine which demands a second, then a third glass can never be a bad wine. The wine of which you cannot finish one glass can never be a great wine.

Ernest Gallo
American winery owner

. . . good wine,
well drunk, can lend
majesty to
the human spirit.

M. F. K. Fisher (1908–1992)
American writer

When I pour a glass of truly fine wine, I hold it up to the light and admire its color. When I raise it to my nose and savor its bouquet and essence, I know that wine is, above all else, a blessing, a gift of nature, a joy as pure and elemental as the soil and vines and sunshine from which it springs.

from *Harvests of Joy* by Robert Mondavi,
American winery owner

Eat, Drink,
and Be Merry

Never save the good stuff for company, you can't take it with you, tomorrow is promised to no man, or as Dad used to say, "Knock it back, kid."

Felice Mancini
Daughter of late American composer
Henry Mancini

Wine is the intellectual part of the meal, meats are the material part.

Alexander Dumas (1824–1895)
French dramatist

In the past, people were always smoking cigarettes in movies. Today, I would hardly imagine a fine dinner portrayed in a movie or a television show that didn't include wine on the table.

Francis Ford Coppola
American film director and winery owner

I feast on wine
and bread, and feasts
they are.

Michelangelo (1475–1564)
Italian artist

In the dining experience, the wine is as important as the food and the music and the art. The first course has to melt into the second course, which has to melt into the next course. It all has to fit together, and wine is part of that.

Steven Chiappetti
American restaurateur

Every time you open a prestigious bottle of wine and share it with friends, it's an extraordinary experience.

Drew Nieporent
American restaurateur

Without good wine, spring is not spring for me.

Hafiz (1325–1389)
Persian poet

My idea of heaven is
to sit in a favorite
restaurant with cheese
and a glass of wine.

Wendy Wasserstein
American playwright

Not only does one drink wine, but one inhales it, one looks at it, one tastes it, one swallows it … and one talks about it.

King Edward VII (1841–1910)
English king

To me, the sensation of drinking a great wine or eating a great meal is the same sensation of having performed well. All this comes from the senses. That's what life is all about.

Maria Tallchief
American ballerina

Wine is the one beverage that is fittingly used to accompany the workman's meal, to observe a memorable occasion, to inspire the poet, to minister to the sick, to welcome, to enhance cooking, to make a banquet perfect, to toast beggar or king. No other beverage has had such universal recommendations throughout the ages.

Leon David Adams
American wine connoisseur

Some of these vintages won't be ready to drink for a long time. If we wait much longer, our kids will be toasting us over our graves! Let's drink up what we have, and let them buy their own.

American actor Burgess Meredith (1909–1997) to film director John Huston (1906–1987)

I grew up with wine on the dinner table. My mother told me we should be able to talk with kings and walk with the common people. So I drink the finest wines when I can—or the worst ones with ginger ale, if that's what's appropriate.

Carol Moseley-Braun
American politician

Matching Wine
with Food

When choosing a wine to drink with your food, it's best to focus on the wine's size and weight. Hearty food needs a hearty wine, because it will make a lighter wine taste weak and insipid. With lighter food you have more leeway.

Lighter wines will balance lighter foods nicely, of course, but heartier wines will show you all they've got. While some say that full-bodied wines "overwhelm" less hearty foods, the truth is that anything but the blandest food still tastes fine after a sip of a heavyweight wine.

I drink wine every day because I adore it and it suits me down to the ground. I really can't eat a meal without drinking wine; it's almost a physical impossibility. I swear I don't digest food as well without it.

Serena Sutcliffe
Head of Sotheby's International
Wine Department

I'm self-taught. I learned about wine by keeping my senses open and learning how it enhances a meal, enhances the whole experience.

Diane Forley
American chef

Wine is not an imperial deity. It is something to drink, something you put in your mouth and sometime later you expel it. But it's bloody marvelous along the way, isn't it?

Len Evans
Australian winery owner

Wine Buying Strategy

When buying a bottle of wine, it's always wise to examine the bottle carefully to make sure that the fill level is good—up to the neck of the bottle—and that wine hasn't leaked through the cork. If wine leaks out, it means that air is getting into the bottle, oxidizing the wine, and spoiling its flavor.

You can't be a wine snob. You have to keep your mind open. You have no idea where the next great wine you drink will come from.

Katy Sparks
American chef

A good meal is wholeness, when everything gels. I like it when everything complements each other, including the wine. That's the way we look at performance—it's the contribution to the whole.

Ramsey Lewis
American jazz musician

There's more to wine than what's in a bottle. It's about having fun, going to food and wine events, and meeting the most exciting people.

Cherry Whitley
American businesswoman

Tasting Tip

The proper way to hold a wine glass is by its stem. Holding the glass by its bowl hides the liquid from view, and the heat of your hand alters the wine's temperature. French enologist Emile Peynaud once said, "Offer someone a wine glass, and you can tell immediately by the way they hold it whether or not they are connoisseurs."

The way wine is made is very much the way food is made; the chef is unique to his own food and style just as the wine-maker is to his wine. I have the same admiration for the winemaker as I do the chef.

Daniel Boulud
French chef

Having wine every night is such a civilized thing. I would like to see everybody enjoy a glass of wine, release their tensions. I'm very fond of the idea of the family meal, complete with wine.

Julia Child
American chef and author

Fish must swim thrice—
once in the water, a
second time in the sauce,
and a third time in wine
in the stomach.

John Ray (1627–1705)
English naturalist

Whenever I taste a wine
I always think of a dish I
want to eat with it. I can
never think of food without wine or
wine without food.

Joachim Splichal
American chef

In Vino Veritas.

Pliny (A.D. 23–79)
Roman naturalist, scholar, and writer

Photography Credits

Black Star:
p. 68 © Steve Murez

Tony Carlson: p. 57

Corbis:
p. 52 © Marko Shark

Gamma Liaison:
p. 101 © Terry Ashe

Paul Godnin: p. 61

Kent Hanson: pp. 30, 38

John Harding: p. 18

International Stock:
p. 41 © Ronn Maratea
p. 42 © Caffee/Photosynthesis
pp. 45, 92 © J. Contreras Chacel
p. 73 © Randy Masser
p. 91 © Philip Wallick

Fred Lyon: pp. 96–97

Jeff Harris: p. 107

Rick Mariani: pp. 2, 46–47, 67, 80, front cover

Sara Matthews: pp. 62, 88

Terrence McCarthy: p. 35

Ted Morrison: p. 10, back cover

Steven Rothfeld: pp. 24–25, 79, 85

Sara Williams: p. 50

Jon Wyand: p. 15

This book has been bound using
handcraft methods and Smyth-sewn
to ensure durability.

The dust jacket and interior were
designed by Frances J. Soo Ping Chow.

The text and photographs were
edited and compiled
by Steffanie Diamond Brown.

Edited by Ann Berkhausen.

The text was set in BeLucian
and Linoscript.